FAKE
IVORY

FAKE IVORY

New and Selected Poems

Marcia Muth

SUNSTONE
PRESS

SANTA FE

Sunstone books may be purchased for educational, business,
or sales promotional use. For information please write:
Special Markets Department, Sunstone Press,
P.O. Box 2321, Santa Fe, New Mexico 87504-2321.

Book and Cover design › Vicki Ahl
Body typeface › Albertus Medium
Printed on acid free paper

———————————————————————————————————

Library of Congress Cataloging-in-Publication Data

Muth, Marcia, 1919-
Fake ivory : new and selected poems / by Marcia Muth.
        p. cm.
   ISBN 978-0-86534-744-1 (softcover : alk. paper)
I. Title.
PS3563.U85F35 2010
811'.54--dc22

                                                2010025226

———————————————————————————————————

Published in

Santa Fe

WWW.SUNSTONEPRESS.COM
SUNSTONE PRESS / POST OFFICE BOX 2321 / SANTA FE, NM 87504-2321 /USA
(505) 988-4418 / ORDERS ONLY (800) 243-5644 / FAX (505) 988-1025

For
Marilyn Fisher and Willard Chilcott
Teddy and Jim Bob Jones
and
Judith Armstrong

In Appreciation for Their Many Years
Of Encouragement and Friendship

CONTENTS

PREFACE

If this was an art exhibit, it would be
called a retrospective. In this book I have
brought together poems from seventy years.
They include favorite poems from previous books
that are now out of print. There are poems from
early literary magazines and other periodicals.
Since poetry is a vital part of my daily life,
there are also new poems.

I

FROM SEASHORE TO RIVERBANK

Why have I, an inland dweller, also always lived by
water in my mind? Was some kind of primordial feeling
for the sea slipped into my DNA? Even as a child, I liked
to pretend that I lived near water and had a little boat.
My first actual experience with a body of water was
with Lake Erie. Both as a small child and a teenager,
summer holidays were spent at Crystal Beach on
the Canadian side of the lake. As an adult,
whenever I traveled to a site near water I would
visit the shoreline or take a boat trip of the harbor.
Now I live in the dry American Southwest, but
my poetry still celebrates the land's waterways.

ON RETURNING TO THE SHORE

Summer unveils the harshness,
Crushing cruelty of winter;
Two trees downed and wrecked,
Someone's lost boat tossed
Up to languish on our shore
But the cottage stands snug
Like a well-anchored ship;
Opening the windows brings
In the smell and sound of sea,
Breezes blow the dust out
To mingle with waiting sand
And slowly fan the pages
Of last year's unread book.

BITS AND PIECES

Walking the shore
In the first light,
I see myself reflected
In the tide pools
That move in the wind
Like small lost lakes.
Last night's storms
Have left bits and pieces
Scattered on the sand;
I step ahead carefully,
A grateful survivor.

SUDDEN STORM

The wind is up again,
Sending waves over rocks
Water inching across sand
Stealing grains, one by one.
The buoy rocks back and forth
Like a crazed carnival ride;
Its bell sending a warning
Answered by shrill creaking
From the shuddering boats
Still tethered to the land.

FOG AT POINT LEON

The fog has crossed the sea
And settled on the land,
Hanging like a gauzy curtain,
Blurring our eyes, blindfolding us
Now, even our voices change
And we speak in soft tones;
The lights in the harbor
Have faded and dimmed
Into wavering shadows
We walk slowly, carefully
Fearful of unseen barriers
Or unexpected chasms;
A longing for the sun
Spreads through our bones.

NORTHERN STORM

The wind-driven northern storm
Has shaken our house and us,
Reworked our familiar landscape
And tossed great slabs of ice
Up on the shattered shore
They are like discarded ice cubes
Draining on the sink board of sand;
We pick our way among the cold debris
Wondering who is holding the sun hostage.

SAFE PASSAGE

Before going to bed
I go to the window,
Looking through the dark
Past the wooden dock
Out to the channel
With its floating lights,
Green and blue guides
For a safe passage
Back into the harbor;
Comforted, I can now sleep.

THE STONY HEADLAND

Standing on the shores of dreams
I see the great ships
Slip past the lighthouse;
Through the mist of time
And a gap of years
I see the piercing light beam
And still hear the buoy bell
Its tone softened by fog.
Much time has passed
Since I last kept watch
By that stony headland
Yet—it stays in my heart.

ONE LAST TIME

The last day at the beach
We build larger sand castles
        Collect more shells
And take longer walks
Letting the seaweed drift
        Around our feet
We stand and sniff the air
        Wanting to remember
The hot sun, the salt smell
        The surf sounds
As waves roll up against us.
Then in evening, after dark
We will dress up and go
        Along the boardwalk
Down to the lights and music
        Of the Dance Pavilion
And later watch the rising moon
Reflect itself in the restless
        Dark night sea.

IN LATE OCTOBER

This is the time to walk the shore
Salt-crazed wind echoes in my ears
Darkened waves roll up and over
Trying to reclaim the summer's land;
Turtles slowly march to hibernation
In the deserted gardens of cottages
Now locked and fettered against
The intrusive hands of winter.

SOUNDTRACK

The wind pushes the waves
Against the rocky shore,
It is a Sisyphean effort
The water returns to the sea
And the endless task goes on,
Its steady pulsing sound
Filled my hours and days;
Now away in another land
It still echoes in my ears.

THERE IS NO FORGETTING

I miss the sea, the endless horizon
The sting of salt on chapped lips
The winter upheaval of ice, storms
And the moodiness of the waves
Sometimes rolling gently toward shore
Sometimes pounding at the rocks
But always demanding our attention;
I marked time by ships and boats
Passing from one harbor to another
On their errands of mystery
And now there is no forgetting
Deep in the marrow of my bones
Foghorns still sound and echo.

RIVER MUSIC

A river runs past my house
Sometimes noisy, filled bank to bank
Sometimes quiet, low and slow-moving
Always there and always changing;
It is my calendar of the seasons,
This river that runs through my life.

Now that it is summer, hot, sunny
The wide river swims with fish
Varicolored scales flashing, looping
In magical, enchanted patterns;
Above the water flying insects
Cling together in hanging clouds
That move along like balloons,
The deep sound of the Bach Suites
Comes from my neighbor's house
While two butterflies dance aloft.

In the autumn leaves fall and float
On the river's surface, going fast
Toward some certain destination
Like a thousand small offerings
Of thanks or beseeching prayers;
The last bird songs are heard
Frogs mourn the passing days,
Cicadas singing predicts winter
My neighbor now plays Elgar
And the wind whispers of melancholy.

Snow covers ground, trees, stones
Standing by the river, I listen
For the familiar sound of water
But the river is ice-bound now
Yet I know that under the ice
The river still flows sluggishly;
My breath-cloud mimics the sky
Overcast, a colorless cloudiness
Then I hear the music of winter,
Creaking of wood in the cold air
Sighing of ice as it forms and re-forms,
The crunching under fast-moving feet
Eager to return to house-warmth.

In the spring winter comes rushing
Down the river's usual course,
Fed by melting mountain snows
And early warm welcoming rains
Little clumps of green appear
All along the water's edge;
There is the joy and sweetness
Of many remembered tiny flowers
Now with windows and doors open
I hear Beethoven spilling out
From my neighbor's house and yard.

II

THE SEASONS

Writing about the seasons is the most natural and ordinary subject a poet could choose. For centuries the importance and effect of the four seasons have been noted and celebrated in the art, literature and music of various cultures and civilizations. Although we may seem to live by a more demanding diurnal clock, we are caught up in the turning wheel of the four seasons.

RENEWAL

At these first signs of spring
We stretch out to the sun
Lifting our faces for benediction.
Tree buds swell and slowly unfurl
Like small flags, filling our eyes
With remembered joy and hope,
Color changes the interstices
Of our space; we feel renewal
Spreading through our veins,
Warming our winter-dry bones.

ONE MORNING

The moon still hangs
In the morning sky;
Blue-smoke hills brighten
Returning the sun's love,
Nighthawks make a last
Lazy circle above the trees
As spring explores the frost away
Exposing grass, rock and root.

THE APPLES OF WINTER

The apples that unheeded
                    dropped and dried
Under the winter sun
Are now swept up in spring's
                    careful raking
Shrunken, patterned, whorled
They are like fossils
Of strange sea-creatures
Yet curiously light
                    to my touch.

SPRING MORNING

Rowing on the river
Crossing from shore to shore
Blades dipping and rising
Wrinkling the water
Where last night's moon
Floated in lonely silence
Now creaking oarlocks
And myriad birds sound
Out our slow coming.

WEATHER WATCH

See how the wind
Has come upon us,
An evil adversary
With animalistic fury
Shaking all the trees
From crown to roots;
Tearing leaves, blossoms
From new spring flowers;
The ark in which we wait
Holds firm and stable,
We are safe if fearful.

LOOKING FOR PROSPERO

These winds that blow
Silencing the birds,
Sending them scurrying
To hidden shelters
Have come unbidden
Over seas and mountains
To wreak havoc on us;
We look for Prospero
To interpret this tempest
That shakes our trees
Stripping away the buds,
Leaving empty twigs.

MAY EVENING

The moon lies like a thumbprint
On the early evening sky
Faint but discernible,
Waiting quietly to begin
The long and lonely patrol
Across the darkened night.

THIS YEAR

Summer was slow in coming,
Trees kept leaves shuttered
Against strong spring winds;
Flowers, grass hunkered low
Loath to leave the comfort
Of winter's warm blanket
Deep soil, old leaves, dreams
Of morning's bright sunlight.

THE SATIE SUMMER

Do you remember that summer?
The cottage on the rocky cliff
Long wooden steps leading down
To the shore, sand, restless sea.
Who could forget those days,
Days of peace when David
Played Satie on the piano.

In the cottage, rooms were large
With darkened corners, ghost-catchers
Years of sand had scoured clean
Window sills and wooden floors.
Pictures were hung everywhere
A grandfather, stolid, stern
Unforgiving, perhaps unforgiven.
A soldier from the last war
Uncomfortable in his uniform
Does he hear our whispers of war
That drift in with the tide?
A picture of a ship slowly sinking
With sailors quickly drowning
Tactless, we think, looking
Out the windows to the sea.
We are uneasy at what we sense
But David at the piano and Satie
Charms all our fears away.

(continued)

We have a treasure hunt
Through the cottage, finding relics
Of previous owners and visitors
Who have paused here for a time
Like shore birds who come and go.
Old magazines, a nature book
One rollerskate, a rolled-up flag
But no diaries, no letters
To give us facts, reliability
David finds an old black coat
Wrinkled, creased with age
He puts it on to play Satie.

In back there is an untidy garden
Its gradual ruin seems inevitable
We all make excuses for it.
In the evening, in candlelight
We sit with our backs to neglect
And face the understanding sea
While David plays Satie on the piano.

BUTTERFLY

Yesterday sitting by the water
And facing into sunlit woods
I counted nine butterflies
Moving gracefully flower to flower
Today I sat very quietly
Still as any earthbound rock
And a butterfly came to me
Resting briefly on my open hand
The moment sweet and too soon over

DO YOU REMEMBER?

That summer we waited for rain,
There were prayers and petitions
There was dancing and drumming;
Still the waves of heat kept
Rolling over the stricken land
While stunted crops turned brittle.
Our bones pushed themselves
Against dry, taut skin;
With dust-filled dimming eyes
We searched the far horizon,
Looking for clouds to break
The parched and arid spell.

FINALLY

Cool air reaches my cheek
                A feather touch
Now at last rain has come,
Breaking this silence of heat
That has hung over our long
                Summer days
Wilting our eyes, our voices
                Dumb with dryness;
Thunder revives, wakes us
                From our sleep.

ODYSSEYS

The morning wind is cool,
Fresh against my face;
It hints of and promises
Days of autumn's ripe color.
On the river, leaf boats
Float slowly on the current;
Bird flock across the sky
Moving like schools of fish,
Now is the time to bale hay.

AUTUMN SCENE

Leaves fall steadily, silently
Covering the picnic area
Filling up the playground
Now there are no more visitors
No children to slide or swing
Birds fly in to reclaim
Their own private kingdom;
By the stone-studded fireplace
A forgotten bag of charcoal
Slowly sheds its paper skin.

IN NOVEMBER

The trees have woven
Their leafless branches
Across the winter sky,
A net of twined twigs
To catch the first snowfall
And hold it captive for us.

WINDFALL

Leaves, wild with the wind
Their colors bright, vivid
In the autumn sunlight
Dance across the walk
Fling against the wall,
Collapsing in quivering piles;
Waiting to be lifted up again
By a drifting tide of air.

GARDEN NOTE

The last flowers of fall
This small stunted hollyhock
Still bravely blooms
In the frost-touched garden.

WINTER WARNING

Suddenly the leaves are gone
Taken by last night's wind,
A warning of winter's coming;
Now I can see the moon
Clearly through the dark
Branches of the old tree.

CHANGING NOW

The hours move more slowly
From light to dark to light
As these wintering months
Shape our day's circles;
No longer guided by the sun
We now follow the moon
Whose crisp whiteness reflects
Crystals of snow and ice.

NOTES FROM THE BLIZZARD

The snow having fallen
For two long days
Has imprisoned us in
Walls and drifts of white,
Crowding out the views
Of our usual world;
Shape-changing the familiar
Sights as a reminder
Of our too easy frailty.

DECEMBER AFTERNOON

Somewhere near a dog barks
But it is mostly quiet now
With new snow frosting
The grass and tree limbs
With careful accuracy;
And laying lightly on the land
Bird tracks map the paths
From hidden nests to feeders
With seed and grain to batten
Their small, thin bones.

IMPRIMATUR

Snow covers the sculpture garden
Making light of the artists' intent
Changing forms, altering designs
Rounding corners, softening limbs.
This new concept intrigues the cat
Who adds his own special marks
Of delicately placed paw prints.

AFTER THE STORM

The stone turtle sleeps
Under the heavy blanket
Of late winter snow;
He dreams of the sun
Warm on his hard shell
And remembers the touch
Of the hands that carved
Him into being and life.

III

BIRDS AND TREES

It is natural to put birds and trees together,
for they have a symbiotic relationship. Birds serve
as harbingers and their sounds are the Greek Chorus
of our lives. Trees are also live anatomical beings. They
grow and change with the seasons from leafy splendor to
stark nakedness. They bend and turn with the wind. They
are defiant survivors of all but the most violent of storms.

KEEPING WATCH

The trees, now black in winter
Stand as sentinels along the road
Like dark shadows come to life
By some magician's wand of hope;
No leaves hiding shapes and gnarls
Their whole being is revealed to us,
Heart and center open to our eyes.

OUR LAST EMPEROR

The raven sits on top
Of our telephone pole,
Raucous, brash and loud;
Glossy black, yellow beak
He is the king of the sky,
Imperious and arrogant.
The pole transforms to totem;
Magic has come to our yard.

INTO THE WOODS AND BEYOND

I write to honor and celebrate
                    Trees
Steadfast sentinels of the land
That holds them captive and close
                    Trees
With furrowed bark, whose signs,
Symbols and runes defeat
Our understanding and cleverness
                    Trees
With branches straight or curved,
Grateful loops of sturdy wood
                    Trees
Whose tender twigs fingerprint
The sky with intricate designs;
With leaves moving, shimmering,
Shaking with each tide of wind
                    Trees
Reminding us that nature lives
And lasts beyond our few years.

RAVEN'S SHADOW

The raven's shadow falls forward
Feathering itself across my heart
Tenderly like green plant leaves;
I hear a pulse, a quiet ringing bell
So soft like the fluttering wings
Of a gilded moth or butterfly,
Raven and I share these moments
Of harmony with all nature.

IN THE MORNING

In the morning after the heavy rain,
The mist rises from the damp grass
Filling the spaces between the trees
And house, an ambient veil that fades
The leaves to a paler color.
The earth gives way beneath my feet
With liquid sounds; I move across
The subdued landscape, seeking a warmth
That only the sun will bring.

RAVENS

Who does not love ravens
Does not love life
Or understand the mysteries
Of our fast spinning planet;
Who does not hear
Whispers of eternity
In a raven's feathered
Flight across the land
Does not know beauty.

FOREST THOUGHTS

Walking through the coolness
Of the tall tree green forest
Moving easily from east to west
I see in my mind the whole earth
A round ball of many colors
Like a planetary Joseph's coat
Revolving slowly around the sun
Keeping time to some secret music.

NEARBY AN OWL NESTS

You have to be silent and still
To see and hear the old mysteries
The small young fir tree clinging
To the side of the deepest canyon
Rocks older than man but more enduring
Little birds flying in big groups
Like schools of fish but skybound.
The sound of raven wings slapping
Softly against the clouded air
Wind that shifts the leaves
And gently lifts your eyelashes
This is a time for remembering
All those forgotten things
While nearby an owl nests.

WINTER VISTA

On the north side
Of the old tree,
The one that winter
Sun rarely touches
There is still snow
Coiled on a lower limb,
Looking from a distance
Like an eyeless snake
Dreaming of a green Eden.

MORAL

The winged bird flies
In all directions,
Seeking and finding
Covering earth's expanse;
Spying out treasures,
Riding tides of winds
And sheltering in tall trees;
The wingless bird sits
And waits for destiny.

THE TWISTED TREE

The twisted tree
Shaped by nature's hand
A reminder of transformation,
An act that comes
To us all in time;
That brittle cedar bark
My own aging hand.

EAGLES

Eagles keep the diurnal watch
Sentries marking off the hours
That men have bound themselves with.
They have chosen not to hurt us,
Not to peck our eyes out,
Or claw our flesh or eat our hearts.
They fly above us, turning, wheeling,
Resting in the taller trees, higher mountains,
Harsh profiles against distant sky;
Free to be envied and sometimes feared.

IV

NIGHTTIME: SLEEPING AND DREAMING

I have always been fascinated by that other world,
nighttime with its dreams. The strange and tantalizing
mix of the real and the surreal, familiar and unexplored
landscapes and known people plus complete strangers.
Sleeping and dreaming is a source of adventure
and even sometimes a place where solutions
to problems have been found.

RHYTHMICALLY

the day divides into its
                natural segments,
morning, noon and night
                not unlike
birth, life and death.
We are forewarned
knowing the natural end,
time and decay to all things
                comes splintering
beyond repair, redemption;
birds don't stop for answers
                nor do we.

ALWAYS

There is a sweet silence
In the after-midnight hours
A time of quiet reflection,
The softening light of the moon
Blurring, enfeebling the lines
And markers of everyday life.

NEAP TIDE

It is the neap tide of night
Darkness has closed down
And arched around us.
I put my hand against the sky
And feel the sharpness of a star.

REFLECTIONS ON THE MOON

Despite our new familiarity
With its rocks and craters
We still revere the moon
Part friend, part fantasy
It has never failed us
Its slow rotation, its phases
The workings of our eternal clock
Always we can take comfort
Knowing that this same light
Shone and still does shine
On Stonehenge, spreading
Its shadows across Salisbury Plain.

ANALYSIS

The secrets of the night
Are kept in our dreams,
Locked away from us
Then slowly released
Like floating balloons
Tempting our grasping hands
Yet always rising above
And beyond our best reaching.

REALITY

At night
sometimes
I know
the meaning
of mortality,
the sharp pain;
my heart
a caged bird;
the realization
of age
but not always
the resignation.

NIGHTFALL

The Tiger of the night
Stalks across the sky,
I lock the doors
Against the dark,
It is time to open
The gate of dreams.

THE THIEF

See how the sun
Has softened the edges
Of my dreams;
Faded the colors I saw.
Dimmed the voices heard
And like a bold thief
Has stolen the magic
Of my nighttime travels.

RITUAL

The morning world
the slow awakening;
the day crawls out
like a turtle hatching
from a sand-buried egg.
A tentative grasp of reality,
black and white become color,
silence becomes sound;
there is no turning back.

RAVEN'S TASK

The raven flies to the east
To raise the curtain of night;
Dreams are slowly eased away,
Oberon has gone to his cave
And we are gently pulled
Forward into morning light.

EACH DAY

When morning returns
Us to our natural state
We greet the world
Glad to be home,
Having been travelers
In the dark nighttime
Country of dreams
And strange adventures
For we are children
Of the sun and live
Only in its light.

DREAM SHADOWS

My dreams float away
Fragile as eggshells
But shadow my days
With little remembrances
Of the night, the people
Who came to visit me;
The great blue bird, the tiger
Their meanings all gone, lost
In the dampening light of day.

V

PLACES AND SPACES

The words place and space have a multitude
of definitions and can be used interchangeably.
To me, "place" means a site, a designated building
or any area where people gather to share in some
common interest or activity.
The word "space" conjures up an intimate
and emotional response. It is a deeper personal
reaction. We all have places of meaning and importance
in our lives, but it is the heartfelt responses
to spaces that we never forget.

MYSTIC CIRCLE

Stonehenge
The past displayed
Though not revealed.
What giant hands
At play there
On Salisbury Plain
Balanced these forms,
Planned the mystic circle
And then left,
Called away
Or bored by blocks
Went home to lunch
Or nap.

CHICHEN ITZA

Oh, the arrogance of ancient monuments
Pitted stone, ruined steps, unroofed rooms
Climbing toward the sun;
Dirt and decay betray your splendor
And in broken waves of crushed debris
I see a warning, mocking reminders
That we are not the first builders.

AT PENASQUE RUINS

Under the midday sun
The ruins of the city shimmer
With illusionary energy;
Leaning against a partial wall,
I sense the lives of those
Whose homes, shops, temples
Made up this circular enclosure
Now surrendered to time.
But while I grieve for the past,
A lizard darts across broken paving
Mocking at my own visible mortality.

OLD HOUSE

The empty rooms
Are abandoned to ghosts
Third-handed from
Unsuccessful dreams
Dust rises, settles
As wood rots, decays;
Doors fall in,
Windows fall out.
Night sounds catch
On the broken glass,
Tear on the nails,
The past cannot
Be truly forgotten.

ON STERLING SQUARE

The old building abandoned
To dust and destruction
By owner and occupants
Left to the light, darkness
Of the natural day and night;
Now marked down
For rubble and reselling
Brick by brick, wood
Windows and doors stacked
In careless uneven tiers.
Each day now, before us
This old building practices
The art of transformation
From one form to another
Becoming finally the newest
"Park Here All Day."

ADMISSION: ONE DOLLAR

Inside the museum
the wax figures pose,
caught in acts
of greatness, violence;
lessons in instant history
like me—unlike me.
Eyes of glass that gleam
but look beyond me;
lips that part
but do not move.
I am uneasy
with these counterfeit forms;
they have secrets
I can never share.

HALL OF THE AMERICAN INDIAN
THIRD FLOOR, NORTH WING

In the museum, I walked through the Hall
Of Indian baskets, weapons, color lithographs
Of the old chiefs, warriors and their horses;
I looked at their proud eyes that trusted
The itinerant artists to record the truth,
Yet the truth betrayed is what covers the face
Of chief and time alike. These are remnants,
Clever symbols locked in and under glass,
"Do not touch" reads the crooked printed sign
But it is now three hundred years too late.

LOS COMPOSANTOS

I walk in these Blessed Fields, the *camposantos*
Not counting crosses but sensing life, years of life
Piled, mounted, saved in wood and stone.
These tipsy monuments carefully carved
Landmarks, pictographs given from man to man,
Eye to mind and then returned again.
Time opened out like a webbed fan;
Acts becoming formed from fixed gestures
Planned in the deeper canals of the mind
Then passed from eye to hand to foot.
And so I, too, make my daily progress
Moving slowly from sea to sky, finally
Dying to an earth I love but cannot save.

AT THE CONCERT HALL

The cello cases, empty
Of their musical selves
Stand straight, upright
Along the backstage wall
Dark, aloof and mute
Like faceless monks waiting
To be called to prayers.

WESTERN UNION DAYS

I pass the Western Union office in the old part of town
not even really commercial, run-down buildings
a pawn shop or two, loan offices, a failed chiropractor,
secondhand clothes shop called "Nearly New"
how optimistic! And, the messages
also nearly new but not quite, mostly spurious
and always emotionally secondhanded.
In the office behind unwashed, cracked plate glass
two people working. Are they actually real?

I can remember Western Union in its glory days
the modern messenger of Zeus riding on a bicycle
with style, flourish; bringing death wishes
from the departed or, words of sickness
or, but rarely, good fortune for the survivors
of others' lives, of life itself.
In those days—take any block of houses
let the Western Union boy ride his way;
see how the curtains twitch, how every eye is glazed,
every pulse slowed to near stop, every breath held.
Where will he go, what dos he bring?
Disaster is most expected; some family will be marked,
lifted out of themselves by that yellow envelope.
A quick catalogue of the sick, the sinking, the old.
Who could it be? Nagging doubts, fears, sudden sweat.
He stops; thank God, not here—or here—but, over
there.

By why there? Curiosity mounts with him
mounting the steep steps, ringing the bell;
the door cracks open, a hand reaches for the mystery.
No tip! He spits on the steps,
looks scornfully at all the closed, silent doors
and rides furiously away out of our lives.

AT THE PHOTOGRAPHY EXHIBIT

Moving slowly from one square
And then to the next square,
From one to another and another;
I am looking through 120 windows
Into rooms of life and death,
Landscapes that cannot change,
Streets pushing toward eternity,
Houses that lean against reality.
I am looking through 120 windows
At strangers who return my timid stare
With the insolence of clever natives.
They are at home, I am an intruder;
A last look shows them still inviolate
While I am changed by viewing
This spectrum torn from time.

THE PARADE

The parade, seen from a distance, seemed small
With figures only matchstick size,
The music thinned in the cold November air.
Watching from a window nearly a block away
We strained to see the floats, to guess their meaning.
The crowd cheered, we saw the float then, the tanks
Big and heavy, out of place on our little streets,
Moving slowly like monsters from old myths;
Suggesting death among the bright carnival colors
And we turned away, shadowed by fear.

WAR MEMORIAL

Who stops now to read the names
Or trade the sharp incised design
Of laurel leaf and crown?
Who remembering that bright dedication
With speeches, flags, music, tears;
Who remembering it will not weep again,
Here where the leaves blow and drag
Themselves against the dusty sign.

AT THE INDIAN PUEBLO

Yesterday I walked where a thousand had danced;
The ground churned to a powdered fineness
And mixed with the ashes of night fires,
Potsherds and broken shells, a subtlety of design.
The sky, an inverted image of the earth
Gave me no sense of well-remembered familiarity.
I was alone with shadow dancers, shadow drums
Except for the watchful dogs who lay
At the edges like guardians of the six directions
And in the windless silence there, I stopped
And heard the brushing sound of time.

THE FEATHER

The ancient Kachinas danced here
Early in the morning, very early,
You can see their footprints
In the dust, soft and fading
Away as the sun comes
One day I found a feather
Where their shadows had been.

THE SET PIECE

Shuffling our feet, stumbling in the dark,
Waiting there, we bent our heads back
And looked the night straight in its eye.
We stood, fixing the sky with such a stare
As if by looking, we could bring to being
That moment of beginning we so desired.

And when that first aerial flower bloomed
Above our heads, we all cried "Ah, Ah";
The sigh of the crowd, a sighing of death in us.
With each flash we felt our secrets wrested from us,
Floating down as hot ashes on our uncovered heads.

Now the final act, that piece of tradition;
Stretched to our limits, standing tiptoe, arm by arm
The smallest lifted up, the oldest held up, waiting.
The match struck home, we drew in our breath
And lost it in the glory of the bright burning
That burned out before our glistening faces.
This was our climax, our act of contrition
Made visible in red, white, and blue.

A TRACE OF SULPHUR

A trace of sulphur on the walk;
The holiday is over, the punk burnt,
The Chinese-pictured red and green
Wrappers crumpled in little balls
Rolled by the wind into odd corners.
The dogs come out of hiding
Sniff the powdered air, walk stiff-legged
To the trees, where the pinwheels were nailed
Spinning out their colors over the night.
In the garden the sparkler wires,
Cooling and denuded of their glory,
Are stuck in random places. They were
Like stars to us in their brief time
And we made them circle, arc and turn
To our pleasure. Now going to sleep
We suck burned fingers, knowing
The trace of sulphur in our patterned lives.

A SPECIAL VIEW

Stopping at the town's edge
And looking toward the west
Through the gap of buildings
You can see the four mesas
Rising up like the knuckles
On some giant's hand.

THIS PLACE

This is where myths are made
Where legends grow like moss
Flourishing in decaying leaves;
This is where dreams are born
And reality splinters into pieces
Like shattered mirror shards
Reflecting only broken images.

VI

UP CLOSE AND PERSONAL

It is true that all poems are personal.
After all, poetry comes from the heart as well
as the mind. However, there are always some poems
that reflect a special happening. They are like the pages
of a secret diary; often the true meaning is hidden in the
net of words. Those poems are a way of remembering
or commemorating an event or experience.

FAKE IVORY

At night my bones
Move slowly
Changing my shape,
Shaping a change.
They are wrapping
Themselves, looping
Around my flesh;
I am encased
In fake ivory.

REFLECTION

Seeing myself in the mirror
I am amused, two of me
Though one is forever kept
Behind the silvered glass
Like a well-preserved exhibit.

DESTINY

Full-flavored and fleshy
The rounded peach
Cupped in my willing hand
Will not last, nor will I,
We are of this moment only
And then become memory.

THE CHILD THAT I ONCE WAS

The child that I once was is still there
Layered by time, covered by more flesh
Bones lengthened, shadowed by the cracks
Of increasing age; muscles slackened.
But inside I carry the child that was me,
Sharing the same hunger, spending our hours
Searching for the right key, the open door
In the long corridor of months stretched into years.

MARCH 5

Today is my father's birthday, I keep it
By a trick of memory, going back
To time and place when we first met
Since fatherhood was long ago broken
On the rack of time and scattered into space.
In the sooted, stone-cracked railway station
My mother held me up above the humming crowd
Swaying in the close press of winter breath
And I, proud to be above the others that way
Felt rooted in a glory that would never pass.
Beyond our seeing, an engine bell rang
Like a buoy off fog wrapped lands
Then at the iron gates like insects fleeing
Some monster predator, a new swarm of faces
Appeared as in a mirror to ours but steamy, unclear
And hands waved quickly on both sides.
Slowly the gates were slid apart by a man
Whose red hat with gold braid I coveted
With all my heart; I reached out, bold
Enough to touch or take when we were shifted
To a lesser view by the crying, moving mob
That pushed and pulled us forward. Someone said,
As I was lifted higher, "There he is, your papa."
And I heard someone laugh in my direction
As I was wrenched from my mother's arms,
Swept up by a new stronger force
Strange father, stranger child; I wept,
My allegiance defected to a gold-braided cap.

CREDO

I am an artist
I cruise the universe
Seeing faces
Selecting images
Like picking out apples
At any handy supermarket.
On a secret journey
I am a silent observer
Visiting neighborhoods
Collecting scenes,
There are no barriers
Between space or time
Everything is unfolded
Everything is understood.

ON FINISHING A NOVEL

I made a mirror of words
And caught my image there;
Should such deceit be framed
Or altered to express consent?
If creation is a six-day bike race
And on the seventh God fell exhausted
Entangled in his spokes of logic,
Shall I renounce my own small effort?

GUARDIAN MOON

I like to walk about the house
In late or middle night
The rooms familiar but shadowed;
Standing by a blinded window,
I peer out at quiet blackness
On the very best of nights
I see the guardian moon
Looking back, we are together
Silent creatures sharing the dark.

AT THE OFFICE

Like fake prisoners in a pretend jail
We eat our little lunches at our desks,
Numbed by the morning's work;
Already intimidated by the future
We chew and swallow, chew and swallow.
Dreams do not exist here, the world is flat
And we sail perilously close to the edge.

PIANO CONCERTO

The music
Washes over me,
I rest
In the notes
Like a bather
Left sleeping
On the shady
Shoreline

AT THE RUMMAGE SALE

Someone's ancestor he must have been, I suppose
Now fourth or fifth-handed cast upon the rummage drift
Of old clothes, books, pictures, assorted dishes
Odd-lotted from the cupboards of dying households;
I buy him for myself with an air of thievery
If my own I do not know, I shall make
My past, like God, in my own likeness as I wish it.

THE CAST IRON BUTTERFLY

Moving again
shelves nearly stripped
bare
like poorly picked bones;
books, hunked flesh
hanging to edges
accenting the emptiness
of unlived rooms.

Most books are packed
neat rows in marked cartons
for the moment dead
gone from touch and other senses.

It takes time to pack books,
I read every third one
pieces of paragraphs
inhaling the words
feeling the text in my pores
remembering other occasions.

Some books, very few
will be left like broken toys
in the deserted playroom
of a yesterday mansion.

Yes, I must move
nomadized by events
computer decreed.

(continused)

Dishes wrapped and ready
for unfolding
archaeologist, I will discover
my china in a new setting.

No chairs left free
I stand at curtainless window
balance a paper cup of coffee;
consider life, life today
instant coffee, instant love, instant death.

I wait
look down at the street
I had meant to walk there
More slowly, more often;
I look at my watch, no time now,
the van will be coming
and as a refugee
I must follow my possessions
down the stairs, across town
across this tired land.

Steam clouds my eyes
the coffee burns;
I taste all goodbyes.

The van turns the corner
I turn away
my heart, a cast iron butterfly.

CEREMONY

The ritual of locking up
A key turns into silence
All that has gone before
Now the absolute settling of dues
Walk away, walk away sorrow
Walk away death, slowly
Things left behind closed doors
Can be more easily forgotten.

OBSERVATIONS

Looking at the photos
Of the distant planet
I see the many craters,
Whitened rims of dryness
Where, perhaps, once lakes
Lapped at the shores;
Mesas of lifted terrain
Whose shadows lay like velvet
On the pockmarked surface
All too far to ever be known
Or touched by our footprints.

AT THE CONCERT

The orchestra starts to play
Time stops then vanishes;
We are caught in a net
Of notes encircling us
We are willing captives
As the music surrounds,
Flowing into our being
And nesting in our hearts.

I RISE EARLY IN THE MORNING

I rise early in the morning
Before street lights have been dimmed
By the moving tide of day.
And standing at a window, watch
The red tinge of sun spread over
Darkened houses and trees. They take form
Become solid, shaped measurable
But in the low pockets of land
Ground fog lingers, concealing
Lesser shapes that cling to the earth.

NEXUS

Spotlighted by the morning sun
A spider's web blocks my path,
I will not disturb its symmetry
I can only admire its perfection;
The careful conjoined strands
A geometry of design hinting
At artfulness and deception.

DARK RIVER

We went into the cave
Following the guide,
Looking back at the light
With intense longing.
"We're going into exile"
Someone whispered loudly,
A nervous laugh that ends
When something streaks across
The low, pitted ceiling.
Silence hangs like a curtain
As we move slowly along
The suddenly narrowed path
Until we enter the cavern
Where a dark river runs.
"There are eyeless fish there"
The guide proudly explains;
We don't turn to look,
We are homesick for the sun.

THE CASTAWAYS

Like Jonah from the whale
We are cast out,
Thrown upon the shore
Of quiet uncertainty;
Left to find our own way
Back to the circle
Of our fondest hopes
Without map or guide,
Yet, we will follow the voice
That speaks within us
Leading back to the center.

GAMES OF CHANCE

How quick we are
To play games of chance
Despite our knowing
About the dealer,
The marked cards, dice
That never win.
We think, we hope;
This time we know
The lucky card
The winning number
Surely, this time
This one last time
It's our turn to win.

I WAIT

I wait
though not patiently;
you are late
and I imagine disaster
like a medieval dragon
has swallowed you up,
leaving me only small bones
when you come, you smile,
breathless and apologizing
for a watch not to be trusted.

LEAVE WORD THAT YOU LOVE ME

Leave word that you love me
I'll find it as I found you.
Leave word in trees, in the bark
In cracked channels of the bark,
Runways of insects whose messages
I can detect but not decode;
I will put my ear to the tree and hear
A pulse of life, a beat of love.
Leave word in the sun
Where its fire touches my skin
I will feel the burn, hurt of love,
The force of life striking at me;
Where my eye cannot look or see
My heart can search and know.
Leave word in fossilized rock
On the cliff by water edge;
I will see, feel the imprint of the past
Petrified into immobility, cast unchangeable.
Leave word in the ocean, that nativity
From which we came, spiraling up to air
To land, to newer freedom, to earth love.
Tree, sun, rock, ocean—on these,
On this love I will build.

VII

VARIOUS AND SUNDRY

As can happen with any project, once the collection
and arrangement is finished it is not really the end.
Often there are some things leftover. In a poetry book
this can be a final miscellany of various and sundry
subjects. They may be philosophical, commentaries on
current events or mind-catching observations on life.
Enjoy this buffet of words.

ALL SYSTEMS GO FOR FIRST FLIGHT
OF NEW SHUTTLE

—Albuquerque Journal

First flight—
Birds leaving nests
Bats flying to dark;
The Wright brothers,
The Montgolfiers
And all other descendants
Of Icarus and Daedalus.
First flight—
Daring and dizziness
Fear of falling, failure
Ecstasy and loneliness
Coldness in bone marrow,
Panic in the blind alleys
Of the skyrocketed mind.
First flight—
Tears of anguish and success.

THE SLOW DESTRUCTION

The fox sits on the edge of the canyon
Listening to the sounds of men,
Witnesses to the slow destruction
Of the western woods, the pond;
Stones torn from the ground,
Hauled away for garden borders.
Each day the line of houses is closer;
One after another the animals leave,
The birds seek new nesting trees.

VISION

The concert over,
Players carry out
Their little black
Coffins of dead music.

QUIET TIME

This is a time of waiting
Quietness, calm
Living in the rounded perfection
Of the present.
Life held captive, motionless
As in a glass globe
Of pure contentment,
Not hunted or hunting.

AFTER LOOKING AT A PAINTING
OF PARADISE LOST

God in his blue uniform
With its gold buttons
Stands at the gate of Paradise
Shouting, "Out! Go!
You have all sinned!"
We leave by twos, laughing
"Leave the Old Man
To his garden, his trees"
We say, not afraid at all
We know there's more to see
More to learn, more to love
In the opened wide spaces
Before our eager eyes and feet.

AMERICAN THEATER—NINETEENTH CENTURY

Those were days of transient magic
Scenery blooming like forced flowers
In a hundred dozen halls, opera houses.

Illyria, Agincourt, and Arden become place-names;
Ophelia dying in rural streams, Hamlet stalking
His father's ghost across country,
The agony of Lady Macbeth, arrogance of Richard
Passing into folklore, remembered long
After sun-peeled posters were picked,
Shredded by spring and summer winds.

THE CITY DREAMS

Beneath the sand, the city sleeps
dreaming of the sea and the sun,
of the time when the tides
rushed between wooden pilings
and ships rested at anchor,
when fruit trees bloomed
and houses were lighted beacons
before the land shifted
and sand covered the shore.

UNDER CONSTRUCTION

This house is not yet a house
though measurements are made,
                squared and known
now it is uprights, beams, joists,
post and lintel, I-beam
                the barest ribs.
I walk around the disheveled earth
thrust aside for this planned encounter
of wood, stone, steel, and dirt,
                calcareous rocks.
Clay has been formed, burned
piled here in a long fort of red;
I balance one brick in my hand,
this is my tie to the past
                to antiquity.
Walking into this framework
its openness like crystal
I see thick green trees
                arched blue sky
in the interstices of the roof;
here where a window will be
a bird flies down to rest.

TRAVELOGUE

The English tea set is gone
Some got chipped, broken
Some sold at last year's sale.
We bought it in London
Along with boxes of tea,
Earl Grey mostly, and now
One cup, handleless, holds clips;
The cat drinks out of the saucer.

MODERN ELEGY

How far away the dead move,
Into some uncharted country
A new Amazon
And, no one writes back
"Having a wonderful time,
X shows where I'm staying."

At first we see them everywhere,
Reflected images
Calling back to us
From shop windows, darkened corners,
Borrowed faces;
Then we forget,
Without reproach or intent
We forget.

ANOTHER CRISIS

In this silence while the world waits
The decision, holding still to hope
How absurd seem our small frights,
Our little economies, out postponements,
This madness of life touches, wounds us
Yet we will survive; love is strongest
When stretched beyond endurance.

NOW WE ARE AS ONE

We have become the inheritors
Of violence-shattered dreams
Rising from smoking ashes;
Now it is for us to create
Bringing out of our sadness
New chords of sounding music
Ringing from heart to heart.

OF MEN AND TIME

The arc of time
                Swings wide
                Swings slow
Its shadow hangs
                Heavy
                Hangs low
And in the vast
                Darkness
                Below
Men scheme and plot
                Eager
                To know
And measure time
                Trying
                To show
How it changes
                Its length
                To grow
How it shortens
                Or checks
                Its flow
Or may sometimes
                Even cease
                To go.

THE RETURNED

I have come back again,
Back from the nameless grave
Over the sea in a dark land.
I have come back again
Because it is spring in my land,
And I love my land and I love spring.
I have come back again
To smell the earth and walk
The even rows behind the ploughman
Whistling as he goes.
I have come back again
To taste the sweetness of spring rain;
To feel the softness of young grass
And to eat of its tenderness.
I have come back to see and feel
The sudden storms of spring . . .
To be pierced by the lightning
And shaken by the thunder,
But always afterward
To be warmed by the sun.
And the children . . .
I have come back to them also,
To watch them at their play
And to hear them speak, sing, and shout.
I love all the children of my land
Because I, myself, once played
In these streets . . . in these fields.

I cannot stay for long,
But I shall come back again often,
Because this is my land,
And I love my land, and its people . . .
. . . and I am lonely.

THE SHADOWHAWK SONGS

1

O, these green forests
Where my heart is hidden
Beneath an old cedar stump
Safe from the lapping
Tongue of time.

2

In the green forest silence
I hear my heart music,
Bell sounds striking softly
Against mossed rocks;
Falling to muteness
On the leaf-covered ground.

3

This was my Pacific crossing
Calm, safe and steady
Riding the tide across;
Homing toward the shore,
Only a nodding friendship
With the whales and seals
That waited outside the land;
Crossing the invisible boundary
I waved goodbye to them
And to the great sea itself.

4

I, Shadowhawk, sit
On the highest totem;
Looking west, I see the past
Looking east, I see the future.
The winds lift my feathers
But gently
Thunderbird flies down from the North
From the land of frozen seas
He does not speak
Together we listen to the sounds
Of the six directions
We rest
But do not sleep;
Day goes into night
Raven cries a warning
Thunderbird and I
Fly away to those we protect.

5

I, Shadowhawk, fly into the dark,
The Shaman's cave
We share, eat seeds
"Now you are stronger."
The Shaman smokes his pipe,
Blows smoke figures, smoke worlds
"This is the past."
Another puff, "This is the future."
A stone falls from the roof,
"This is the present."
He offers me a blue bead
"See, all the sky here and the sea."

I swallow the bead
"Now you are wiser
Go to those who ask
Speak to them in their dreams."

6

I feel the tides
In my blood, the heartbeat
Of a living planet
Yet I know if I fly high,
Higher than a whale's back
Higher than before, I will see
The tides are the shuttle
Of the giant weaver, the one
Called Fate's Handmaiden,
She makes the great tapestry
Intricate patterned history.

7

I fly to the Stone City
The gatekeeper comes with a lantern,
He wears an owl headdress
Masks hang on the walls,
Some move
Some are sightless
When they speak it is low
Like far-off thunder
But it is in their silence
That the truth is heard.

BIRTHDAY GIFT

Becoming ninety makes a difference,
Like turning an unknown corner
Or crossing a strange threshold;
There are new possibilities, choices.
Now Nature becomes a closer friend,
Bird songs are suddenly sweeter,
Leaves whisper their secrets,
Trees share their years with us.
An inner clarity of contentment
Marks and traces our hours.